EARTH to EDEN

AUDREY CROUCH

T0016813

ILLUSTRATED BY DOMINIKA RENSCH

Trilogy Christian Publishers
A Wholly Owned Subsidiary of Trinity Broadcasting Network
2442 Michelle Drive
Tustin, CA 92780

Copyright © 2023 by Audrey Crouch

All Scripture quotations, unless otherwise noted, taken from THE HOLY BIBLE, NEW INTERNATIONAL VERSION, NIV Copyright © 1973, 1978, 1984, 2011 by Biblica, Inc. Used by permission. All rights reserved worldwide.

All rights reserved, including the right to reproduce this book or portions thereof in any form whatsoever.

For information, address Trilogy Christian Publishing
Rights Department, 2442 Michelle Drive, Tustin, Ca 92780.

Trilogy Christian Publishing/ TBN and colophon are trademarks of Trinity Broadcasting Network.

For information about special discounts for bulk purchases, please contact Trilogy Christian Publishing.

Manufactured in the United States of America

Trilogy Disclaimer: The views and content expressed in this book are those of the author and may not necessarily reflect the views and doctrine of Trilogy Christian Publishing or the Trinity Broadcasting Network.

10 9 8 7 6 5 4 3 2 1

Library of Congress Cataloging-in-Publication Data is available.
978-1-63769-806-8
978-1-63769-807-5

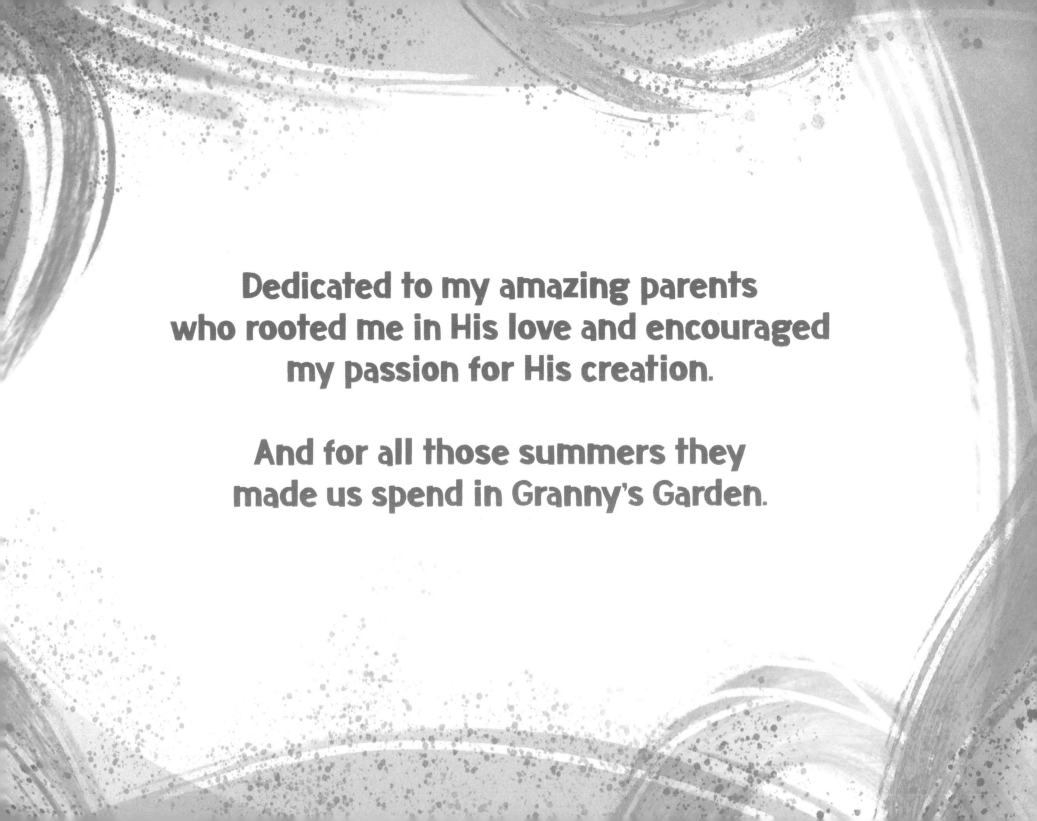

Dedicated to my amazing parents
who rooted me in His love and encouraged
my passion for His creation.

And for all those summers they
made us spend in Granny's Garden.

Eden wakes up on a
day like any other,
with a jump out of bed
and a world to discover!

She runs down the stairs to
breakfast in the kitchen.
Dad brings over pancakes and
a story if only she'll listen.

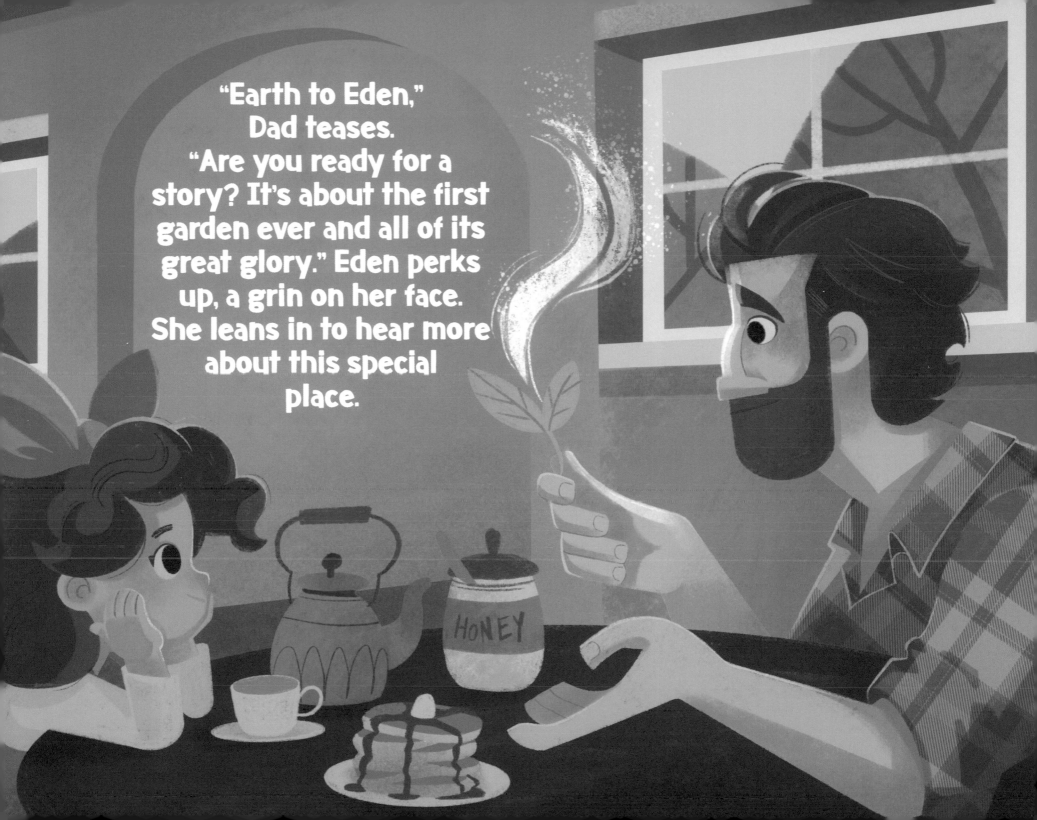

"Earth to Eden,"
Dad teases.
"Are you ready for a
story? It's about the first
garden ever and all of its
great glory." Eden perks
up, a grin on her face.
She leans in to hear more
about this special
place.

"Well," begins Dad,
"this garden was perfect,
as beautiful as could be.

There were trees and
streams and animals
as far as one could see.
A great Gardener - like no
other - planted this garden to
perfection. It was glorious
and He looked on with
great affection.

Two helpers lived there too, named Adam and Eve. They were a little like us if you can believe. They helped with the garden, caring for His creation. It was their care and His love that built the foundation.

The garden was full of life with the birds and the beasts. Adam and Eve were happy and could have all the fruit feasts. But there was one powerful tree full of fruit to avoid, the Gardener warned. If they ate from this tree all would be destroyed.

Adam and Eve fell short and
gave into the fruit's lure.
They ate the fruit and were
no longer pure. The pair had to leave
the garden, paying quite a big price.
For if they didn't, it would no longer
be a perfect paradise."

The story is over and Eden
runs out to catch the big yellow cheese.
Through the window she thinks of the
garden compared to what she now sees.

The bus passes concrete castles
filling the sky with gray.
She sees crumbled up litter
along the way.

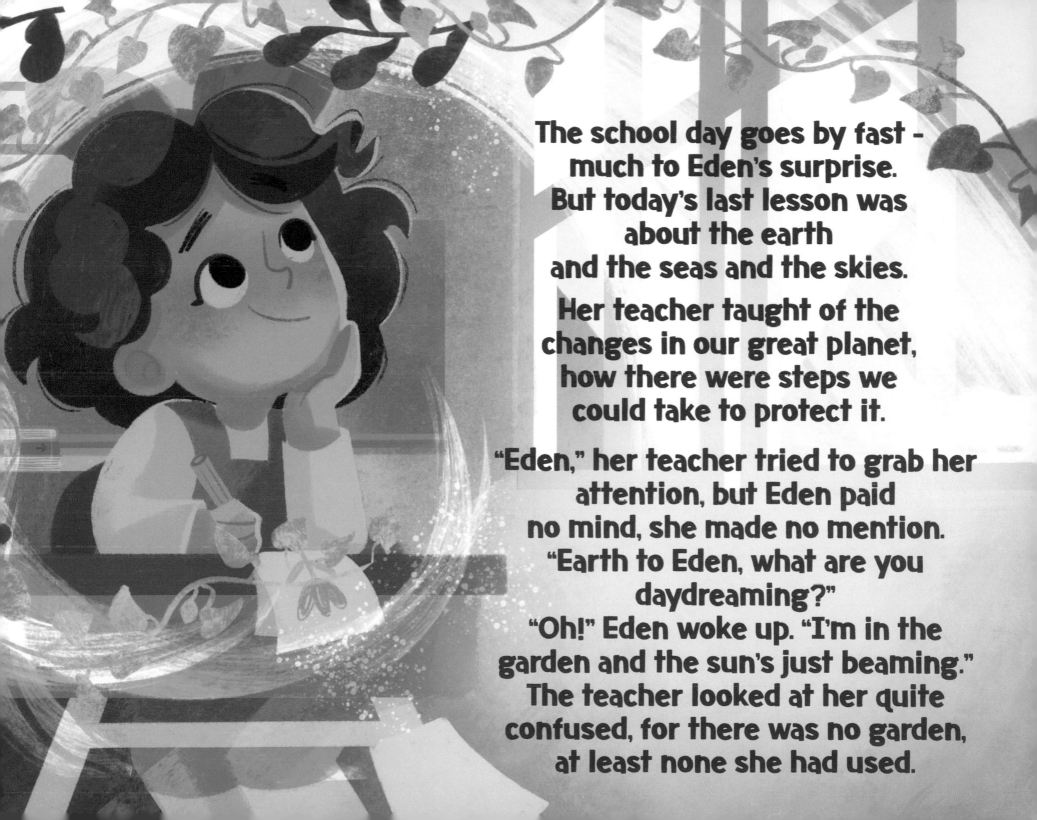

The school day goes by fast –
much to Eden's surprise.
But today's last lesson was
about the earth
and the seas and the skies.

Her teacher taught of the
changes in our great planet,
how there were steps we
could take to protect it.

"Eden," her teacher tried to grab her
attention, but Eden paid
no mind, she made no mention.
"Earth to Eden, what are you
daydreaming?"
"Oh!" Eden woke up. "I'm in the
garden and the sun's just beaming."
The teacher looked at her quite
confused, for there was no garden,
at least none she had used.

Eden decided to share her dad's story of the great garden paradise. The teacher chimed in with some encouraging advice:

How to care for our trees, the bees, and the fruit.
How to tend to our lands, our gardens, to the very root.

The school day ends just as it would, but Eden is stuck in her head, in that garden, wanting one of her own if she could. She gets on the bus pondering, the garden then, and the earth now. She arrives home needing some help and, of course, Dad knows just how.

Together they plant a bountiful garden: veggies, fruits, and flowers. They can't wait to watch it grow after the first rain shower.

Weeks and weeks go by, their garden growing by the day. Eden cares for each plant in her own special way.

The garden fills with little creatures and tiny bugs - bees, birds, and bunnies, even slimy slugs. It is finally time to harvest the garden's bounty. Dad and Eden look over the riches quite proudly.

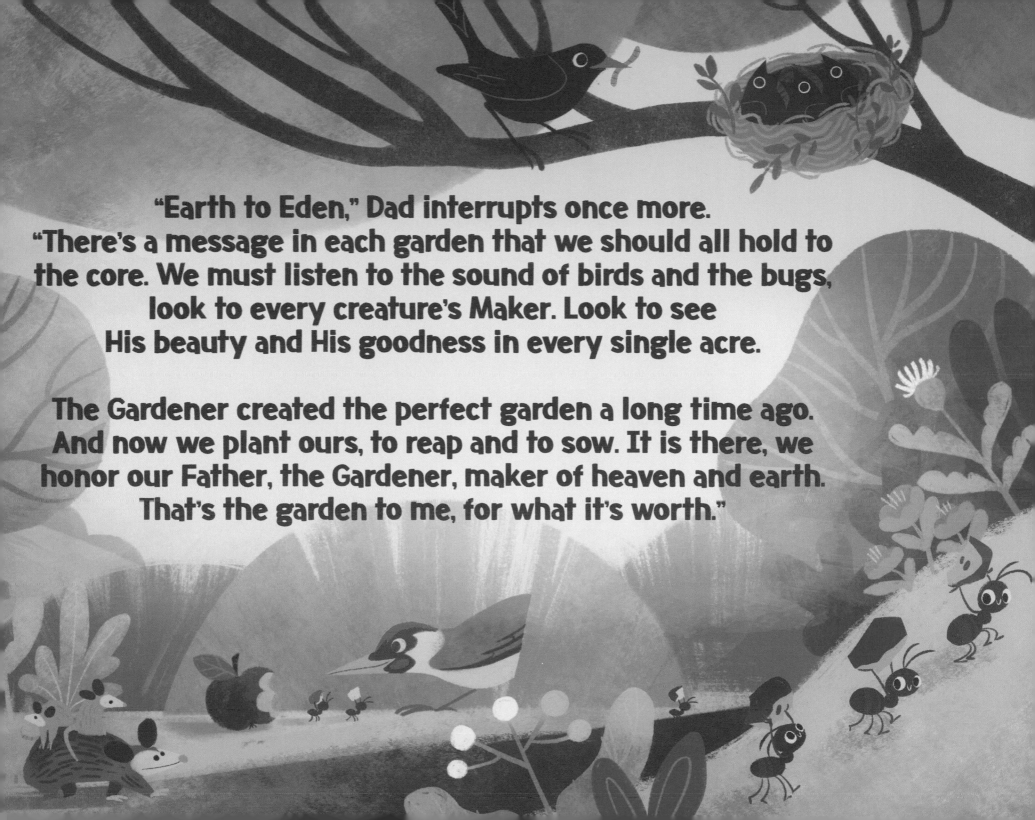

"Earth to Eden," Dad interrupts once more.
"There's a message in each garden that we should all hold to
the core. We must listen to the sound of birds and the bugs,
look to every creature's Maker. Look to see
His beauty and His goodness in every single acre.

The Gardener created the perfect garden a long time ago.
And now we plant ours, to reap and to sow. It is there, we
honor our Father, the Gardener, maker of heaven and earth.
That's the garden to me, for what it's worth."

Eden listens carefully, absorbing
all of Dad's words.
"He made everything wonderful,
from the fruits to the birds.
He created all of the land and the
deep ocean blue, but most
importantly He created something
as special as the garden: you!"

The end.